Mar

Happy

Birtha

love

Kim

H.x.

D0262252

Flowers
For
My Friend

Compiled by
Christina M. Anello

Design by Michel Design

PETER PAUPER PRESS, INC.
WHITE PLAINS · NEW YORK

For my sister, Marisa

Copyright © 1992
Peter Pauper Press, Inc.
202 Mamaroneck Avenue
White Plains, NY 10601
All rights reserved
ISBN 0-88088-757-5
Printed in Hong Kong
7   6   5   4   3   2   1

FLOWERS FOR
MY FRIEND

*E*ver since I could
remember anything, flowers
have been like dear friends to
me, comforters, inspirers,
powers to uplift and to cheer.

CELIA THAXTER

The only rose without thorns is friendship.

MADELEINE DE SCUDERY

True friends, like ivy and
  the wall
Both stand together, and
  together fall.

THOMAS CARLYLE

*F*lowers leave some of
their fragrance in the hand
that bestows them.

CHINESE PROVERB

...*N*obody sees a flower—really—it is so small—we haven't time—and to see takes time like to have a friend takes time.

GEORGIA O'KEEFFE

*L*ove is like the wild
rose-briar;
   Friendship like the
   holly-tree.
The holly is dark when the
rose-briar blooms,
   But which will bloom most
   constantly?

EMILY BRONTE

Gather ye rosebuds
while ye may,
    Old Time is still a-flying,
And this same flower that
smiles today
    Tomorrow will be dying.

ROBERT HERRICK

A hundred persons
turned together into a
meadow full of flowers would
be drawn together in a
transient brotherhood.

HENRY WARD BEECHER

*S*ome friendships are
made by nature, some by
contract, some by interest,
and some by souls.

JEREMY TAYLOR

I have here only made a
nosegay of culled flowers,
and have brought nothing of
my own but the thread that
ties them together.

MICHEL DE MONTAIGNE

For, lo! the winter is past, the rain is over and gone; the flowers appear on the earth; the time of the singing of birds is come, and the voice of the turtle is heard in our land.

SONG OF SOLOMON 2:11, 12

Friendship is a sheltering tree.

SAMUEL TAYLOR COLERIDGE

True friendship is like a rose: we don't realize its beauty until it fades.

EVELYN LOEB

Certainly, flowers were pleasant to the eye. Such things had even their sober use, as making the outside of life superficially attractive, and thereby promoting the first steps towards friendship and social amity.

WALTER PATER

When friendship once
Is rooted fast
It is a plant
No storm can blast.

From a 19th-Century Calling Card

riends are like melons.
Shall I tell you why? To find
one good, you must a
hundred try.

CLAUDE MERMET

*J*une reared that bunch
of flowers you carry,
From seeds of April's sowing.

ROBERT BROWNING

*T*o cultivate a Garden is to walk with God.

CHRISTIAN BOVEE

*A*n old friend can be a
garden of true delight.

NICK BEILENSON

Die when I may, I want it said of me by those who know me best, that I always plucked a thistle and planted a flower where I thought a flower would grow.

ABRAHAM LINCOLN

A friend may well be reckoned the masterpiece of nature.

RALPH WALDO EMERSON

O friend! O best of
friends! Thy absence more
Than the impending night
darkens the landscape o'er!

HENRY WADSWORTH
LONGFELLOW

What's in a name? That
which we call a rose
By any other name would
smell as sweet.

WILLIAM SHAKESPEARE

*S*he asked him but to
stand beside her grave—
She said she would be
daisies—and she thought
'Twould give her joy to feel
that he was near.

ALEXANDER SMITH

Small service is true
service while it lasts.
Of humblest friends, bright
creature! scorn not one:
The daisy by the shadow
that it casts,
Protects the lingering dew
drop from the sun.

WILLIAM WORDSWORTH

*P*lant a seed of friend-
ship; reap a bouquet of
happiness.

LOIS L. KAUFMAN

*F*ame is the scentless
sunflower, with gaudy
crown of gold;
But friendship is the breathing
rose, with sweets in
every fold.

OLIVER WENDELL HOLMES

The hyacinth's for constancy with its unchanging blue.

ROBERT BURNS

The dependable daisy is a
good friend in all weather.

JOHN P. BEILENSON

*I*f you truly love Nature,
you will find beauty
everywhere.

VINCENT VAN GOGH

*E*ach flower possesses its own uniqueness as does each friend.

BETH JAYKUS

What sunshine is to flowers, smiles are to humanity. They are but trifles, to be sure; but, scattered along life's pathway, the good they do is inconceivable.

JOSEPH ADDISON

The least flower, with a
brimming cup, may stand
And share its dew-drop with
another near.

ELIZABETH BARRETT
BROWNING

We have been friends
    together
In sunshine and in shade.

CAROLINE E. S. NORTON

*H*appiness is to hold
flowers in both hands.

JAPANESE PROVERB

*B*ut as some lone
  wood-wandering child
Brings home with him at
  evening mild
The thorns and flowers of
  all the wild,
From your whole life O fair
  and true,
Your flowers and thorns you
  bring with you!

ROBERT LOUIS STEVENSON

*R*egard a friend's
sharp tongue as you would a
rose's thorn.

LOIS L. KAUFMAN

Don't touch my
plumtree!
Said my friend
And saying so . . .
Broke the branch for me

TAIGI

True friendship is a plant of slow growth, and must undergo and withstand the shocks of adversity, before it is entitled to the appellation.

GEORGE WASHINGTON

*H*eigh ho! sing heigh
ho! unto the green holly:
Most friendship is feigning,
most loving mere folly;
Then, heigh ho! the
holly!
This life is most jolly!

WILLIAM SHAKESPEARE

Friendships begin with liking or gratitude—roots that can be pulled up.

GEORGE ELIOT

If I am wrong,
my friend,
please tell me
So I won't
reap a harvest of weeds.

JIM BEGGS

A loving heart carries with it, under every parallel of latitude, the warmth and light of the tropics. It plants its Eden in the wilderness and solitary place, and sows with flowers the gray desolation of rock and mosses.

JOHN GREENLEAF WHITTIER

With a health to the
Cedar—the Evergreen
King—
Like that Evergreen so may
our friendship be.

ELIZA COOK

*I*f instead of a gem, or even a flower, we should cast the gift of rich thought into the heart of a friend, that would be giving as the angels give.

GEORGE MACDONALD

A good garden may
have some weeds.

PROVERB

*C*ultivate your friendships
as you would your garden.

NICK BEILENSON

*E*arth laughs in flowers.

RALPH WALDO EMERSON

*H*e that plants trees
loves others besides himself.

THOMAS FULLER

*F*lowers always make people better, happier, and more helpful; they are sunshine, food and medicine to the soul.

LUTHER BURBANK

Won't you come into my garden? I would like my roses to see you.

RICHARD SHERIDAN

In the city fields
Contemplating
Cherry-trees . . .
Strangers are like friends

ISSA

*S*end flowers to the
living, not to the dead.

EVELYN LOEB

I never cast a flower
away,
    The gift of one who
    cared for me—
A little flower—a faded
flower—
    But it was done
    reluctantly.

CAROLINE ANNE SOUTHEY

*B*ut friendship is precious, not only in the shade, but in the sunshine of life; and thanks to a benevolent arrangement of things, the greater part of life is sunshine.

THOMAS JEFFERSON

They spring to cheer the
sense and glad the heart.

ANNA LETITIA BARBAULD

When words escape us,
flowers speak.

BRUCE W. CURRIE

Flowers grow out of dark moments.

CORITA KENT

*S*ay it with flowers.

PATRICK O'KEEFE

*F*lowers and children—
emblems meet,
Of all things innocent and
sweet.

MARGUERITE BLESSINGTON

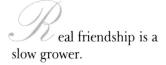

eal friendship is a
slow grower.

Good Manners

*H*alf the pleasure of
enjoying the beauty of spring
is being able to share our
observations with a friend.

EVELYN L. BEILENSON

*T*wo lovely berries
moulded on one stem:
So, with two seeming bodies,
but one heart.

WILLIAM SHAKESPEARE,
A Midsummer-Night's Dream

Hawaii is the only place
I know where they put
flowers on you while you are
alive.

WILL ROGERS

I thought I was alone;
then someone sent me
flowers.

CHRISTINA ANELLO

*B*est friend, my well-
spring in the wilderness!

GEORGE ELIOT

The world is so empty if one thinks only of mountains, rivers and cities; but to know someone who thinks and feels with us, and who, though distant is close to us in spirit, this makes the earth for us an inhabited garden.

GOETHE